Monkey Tricks

Lauren French

Grosvenor House
Publishing Limited

This book is published by
Grosvenor House Publishing Ltd
Link House
140 The Broadway, Tolworth, Surrey, KT6 7HT.
www.grosvenorhousepublishing.co.uk

This book is a work of fiction. Any resemblance to
people or events, past or present, is purely coincidental.

A CIP record for this book
is available from the British Library

ISBN 978-1-80381-292-2

Acknowledgements

Thank you to all my loved ones for the inspiration, encouragement and support they've given me to write this book. In particular to my beautiful wife Naomi, my boy Arlo, my loving parents Catherine and Alan, my Nin Nin, my brother and sister-in-law Russ and Jade, my best friend James and of course, my wonderful in-laws; Simonne, Rod, Oli and Dani. Thank you all, it's been an adventure!

Chapter One

"Hey little Lou,

Don't worry, things will make sense as you get older. Growing up isn't easy for you, but it makes you who you are. You'll learn a lot about yourself, and right now you should be so proud of who you are and who you will become. I guess I'm writing this letter to you to try and help with some of the difficult things you're feeling and going through right now.

The reason you feel sick and have nightmares sometimes is because (and you won't realise it just yet), that you suffer from something called anxiety. Anxiety ~~is a bitch~~ can make you feel afraid and worry about all sorts of things. You have like, an imaginary monkey in your brain that tells you to be scared at times when you actually don't need to be. It worries a lot about you because it wants to keep you safe and protect you, and that's a good thing. But remember, monkeys are ~~pricks~~ wild animals and sometimes that means you have to try your best to tame them to stop them from playing tricks on you. It can be really scary and that's why we have our pink bear. Pink bear still

1

helps us now, even as a grown-up! I still cuddle pink bear every day and he always makes me feel better. It's important to have things that make you feel better. ~~Like gin.~~ I'm still working hard now to train our imaginary monkey, ~~fucking thing~~ but practice makes perfect!

So I know school for one, is hard. Some kids say a lot of really mean things to you and sometimes leave you out. They laugh at you for silly things and for stupid reasons, but it's important to know - you've done *nothing* wrong. It's never deserved and you aren't different to anyone else, even though they tell you that you are. This is probably because they're insecure with themselves, jealous of you, or just plain ignorant ~~(or just *massive* dicks)~~. Sometimes I know that you can treat others badly too, but mostly because you don't know how to process your hurt right now. At times, you find yourself in such a sad and lonely place, but things get better when you realise you have the best family ever! And from these experiences, you learn to make 'fairness' one of your core values, which is a really important quality to have. You'll make a lot of different friends in school, and you'll lose a few too, ~~good riddance~~ but this is okay, and completely normal; you need to find 'your' people, the ones that will make you feel happy and safe ~~and that will drink gin with you~~. Despite your not-so-good experiences throughout school, you still choose to stay for higher education in hope of getting a good job ~~(but, spoiler alert; you~~

~~don't~~). You're worried because you don't really know what you want to do, but that's okay because no-one really does. You'll eventually discover your love for art and music, and guess what? You learn to play the guitar! You even teach yourself! How amazing is that! One of the things I love most about you is your determination. If you really want something, you give your all to get it. Both art and music become really important 'vents' in your life ~~(as does screaming in your car)~~, they make you feel happy and content. One day you'll go on to write your own songs and play gigs in front of lots of people! You're SO brave, and talented. Your songs are amazing!

You'll realise one day that you fancy girls, not boys. For some time you'll try to deny it, because it's just one more thing that makes you feel different, and I know right now, 'different' is exactly what you don't want. You believe that being different makes people mean. But not all people, and not always. Just remember how brave you are and your amazing family help you to feel better too. They really will. You come to realise that feeling accepted and supported is so important for you. And someday, you'll also realise that 'different' is actually a really good thing.

I can't lie to you; you'll find relationships pretty hard to begin with. You'll naively throw yourself into them in hope to find love, which is all well and good, but you need to make sure to protect yourself too when doing so. For some reason you always believed that being in a relationship is the most important thing in life and you have to have it in order to feel whole - like you're *someone*. But this isn't true. You are your own person and you should always put yourself first. Sometimes others will let you down, make you feel unworthy and rejected, like you want to die. You'll most likely experience the worst hurt you've ever felt before. You'll start to not recognise yourself and it'll feel like you're losing yourself. At times you may start to believe that this is normal and that you deserve to be treated in that way. But you absolutely DON'T. Be true to you, look after you and you'll find that things *will* get better, again, with thanks to your people. And guess what? That fairy-tale happily-ever-after you've always wished for? You get it! And it's the best thing EVER!

As I near the end of my letter, I just want to tell you how sorry I am. I realise that I need to take my own advice and stop giving myself such a hard time, because I owe it to you, little Lou, to treat myself better now, because I deserve it. We deserve it. I was learning, I made mistakes and that's okay. I forgive me.

I love you,
Big Lou"

Chapter Two

Oh my god, I've done it, I've FINALLY done it. After several attempts of starting, stopping, and starting all over again, the letter I've been trying to write is DONE! I'm practically a hero to my younger self... If only I could transport back in time with this letter and show it to myself...

I mull this idea over for a brief moment until a sudden revelation hits me. I immediately stand to attention (causing minimal head-rush), throw my arms in to the air and announce to my empty house; "I could build a time machine and... shit!" I look down and realise as I celebrated my completely unrealistic notion that I spilt my beloved gin all over me. I immediately pour another out of shock and then think that this task was probably better done sober. But it's been so hard to do and I'd been putting it off for months, so really, it was now or never.

I re-read my letter and wonder if my shrink would approve. I sit back down and find myself voicing out loud (again); "my poor younger self, she had *no* idea what was coming her way."

The sheer weight of that spoken thought forces me to literally nose-dive into the dome of my gin glass.

I know I *shouldn't* drink, but no-one's here right now to tell me off. My wife is currently out of the country, travelling around some jungle somewhere. She's so much more adventurous than I am. And she *hates* alcohol, so with her away, I can drink all the gin I like!

She's a very patient woman, my wife Nicole. And beautiful too. She has long, wavy red hair and honey-brown eyes. She's slight and very tall; she towers of my mere five-foot-average height. I, on the other hand, am considerably more plump, with green eyes and short mousey-brown hair. I hate that description; 'mousey', how on earth does that describe a hair colour? I completely, and accidently, squashed a mouse once and it didn't look anything like my hair, but then it had been dead for a few days before I found it. My Dad affectionately calls me the 'mouse-murderer' now, but I didn't mean to do it, I swear! Anyway, my point is, we are quite the opposite of each other, and maybe that's why it works so well.

We met at a bar, which I know sounds unlikely, as Nicole doesn't drink. But my local pub, on this particular night, thought they'd try their hand at a bit of culture and put on a 'spoken word' evening. Which Nicole loves. She'd always enjoyed listening to spoken word poetry, with a dream of hers being to actually perform her own someday. And that day was the day. The moment she stepped on to that stage, which was actually just a bit of space the bar staff made in front of the old fire-place, I knew. It was like slow-motion, as if my brain had considerately slowed the moment right down so I could take in its every perfect detail. But, it likely was mostly nauseousness from the amount of liquor in my system at that point. Either way, I'm grateful it happened. For someone that's normally so confident, she was entirely vulnerable in that moment. I didn't know her then, but I *saw* her. And I fell in love with her in a way I never thought possible. Like the love you see in the movies, this normally unrealistic depiction of love at first sight was really happening. I was mesmerised throughout her performance and I was completely blown-away. She spoke of life truths that everyone could relate to, but things that no-one would ever actually say. She was so brave and fierce. I was completely taken over. At the end of her recital she looked straight at me and smiled. I couldn't believe *she* noticed *me*. And that's how she and I became we.

I drop the letter on the floor next to me and slump further in to my old vintage rocking chair. As I start to pacify myself with its gentle rhythm, I run my index finger in to a familiar groove in the arm and close my eyes. All that writing seems to have made me tense. I don't really like thinking about the past. But I've been told I need to understand and accept it to move forward, so that's what I'm trying to do. I just don't know how I managed to write as positively as I did about it all, seeing as I don't see any of it as particularly positive at the time. I feel a bit like a liar, a fraud.

I know some of what I've written is professional advice I've actually been given, but I'm merely reciting the language, not understanding it. I hope when I go back in time with my imaginary time machine that my younger self won't see through my heavy scribbles and laugh. But the jokes on you, little one, you've got allll of this to come! I take another huge gulp of gin and almost immediately pass out.

Chapter Three

I wake with the most horrendous pounding in my head. What on earth is that ungodly noise?! I reach for painkillers, which drunken me so thoughtfully left out for future hung-over me last night and I take them appreciatively. Oh I wish that noise would stop. I look down and see it's coming from my phone, my friend Jack is trying to call me. What the fuck Jack, it's like 7am! As a knee-jerk reaction I launch it in to the next room and groan a sigh of relief. After my skull stops trying to rip itself apart, I get up and haul myself to the kettle. I am going to need a lot of sugar in my tea this morning. After my third sip I realise the actual time from my louder-than-usual tick-tocking kitchen clock, which in actual fact, says 11:35am. Oops. As I watch the clock tick its next tock I remember the letter I wrote last night. I thought I was supposed to feel better after writing it, but now all I can think of is how I could've done things differently in my life. I go back to the front room, pick it up off the floor and just watch it for a few minutes in hope that some sort of epiphany will hit me and I'll be magically cured. But it doesn't. Frustration jabs at me, so I find my phone, which is propped up against the 'important documents' cupboard (everyone has one of those, right?) in the study and start a new text;

'Hi Sam. I know it's been a while, but I finally did that letter you asked me to. It's not made any difference though. Can we meet to discuss it? Thanks, Louise'.

I can't believe I used to pay this woman so much money, I thought she had all the answers, why couldn't she just fix me?! I sit for a few minutes day-dreaming in to the glare of my phone, until a reply comes through, startling me and bringing me back to the land of the living;

'Hi Louise, no problem, how about next Wednesday, 4pm? Sam.'

My heartbeat has become more apparent and my palms already feel sweaty. Maybe it's the alcohol. Maybe it's that damn monkey. Either way, I'm struggling to concentrate on her reply. I manage to eventually compose myself and simply reply with;

'Yes that's fine, thank you. See you then. Louise.'

I already feel unsettled, and not just because I'm fighting this horrible hangover. I know I want to go, I have to, but I'm afraid to. I find myself talking out loud again, which I do a lot whilst I'm on my own, ah, who am I kidding, I do it a lot when I'm not on my own too! I'm instantly reminded of Nicole and I start to smile, she told me once that she didn't realise just how much I talked to myself until we started living together. Makes me sound crazy! But I think it really helps me to process things better. It's also supposed help me to 'normalise my reactions', or so I've been told. Reasoning with myself has always been my favourite past-time anyway. That should be all I need to do today? I think I deserve a rest.

Chapter Four

I can't stand monkeys, which is oddly ironic as I supposedly live with one in my head. Makes sense I suppose, my emotions can be pretty erratic at times. My monkey doesn't like Sam *at all*; it doesn't like to be tamed. It just wants to cause chaos in my head.

At first, when Sam told me I have a monkey in head, I thought *she* was the crazy one. However, what I've come to learn is, monkeys are primitive, instinctual, as is the 'back part' of our brains, hence the bizarre metaphor. It's something to do with the release of adrenaline when there's 'danger' in sight, well apparently my monkeys afraid of EVERYTHING. Even something as simple as texting Sam, it feels instantly threatened and wants to attack. Poor Sam.

Sometimes when I try and 'tame' my monkey (by listening to it and trying to reason with it), I can almost feel it running circles around me, laughing at me. And oddly, it can be terribly amusing. I know I shouldn't be amused by it though. Serious, Lou, serious. Sometimes it does let me win and settles itself back down, so I guess some of the work I've been doing isn't completely hopeless. I still feel sick at the thought of going to the centre next week though to talk over my letter. Terrifying.

"Where on EARTH have you been?!" I hear a loud banging and instantly jolt upright letting out a little shriek in the process (and maybe a little wee too...) – DANGER DANGER – great, and now the monkeys roused. I shake my head, take a deep breath in and turn around to face the direction of the familiar, yet slightly terrifying voice.

"Jeez, Jack", I exhale, "hello to you too!"

"I've been worried sick Lou, not knowing where you'd disappeared off to!"

Jack sounds pretty worried, but his face says otherwise. He's used to me 'disappearing' for a few days. And everyone knows, when I say disappearing, I really mean avoiding. No escaping this one though, he's stood at the window of my front room looking in with his hands curving around his eyes like binoculars.

"Hardly disappearing if I'm at home Jack, glad you didn't send a search party" I snort.

He shakes his head. "Anyway", he finally says, "will you let me in?"

I'm not really feeling up to having any company, but I decide to agree nonetheless. I feel exhausted a lot of the time and my friends just think it's because I'm nearing my mid-thirties. Bastards. But it has been a while since I've seen Jack, so.

"Of course", I say begrudgingly as I saunter towards the front door, trying to clear away the old take-away wrappers from last night along on the way.

I finally pull the door open and am instantly regretful. The blinding laser-like rays of sunlight slice through me and I can't help but wince away in disgust.

"Wow heavy night was it, why wasn't I invited?" Jack sounds genuinely gutted. He can't understand, as the 'professional' near-alcoholic that he is, that someone else can get drunk WITHOUT him. How obscene!

"I had some stuff to do Jack, maybe next time?" I reply.

"Humph. Well, anyway, I'm here to ask a favour", he continues. Surprise, surprise. Just once in my life I wish I could be the one to 'ask a favour', it's always take, take, take with him, and I can't give, give, give that much right now. Another thing I learned in therapy… 'You cannot give what you do not have; you must make sure *your* cup is full first'. I don't even *know* where my cup is right now, but I know it's probably dried up somewhere, like my still hairy, morning-after-the-night-before tongue.

"What is it?" I eventually reply. And gesture him a seat in the front room, quickly grabbing my leftovers off of it before he plants himself in to it unknowingly.

"Well, I need you to cover for me at work. I'm going on a date next Wednesday afternoon with that girl I like from Anavrin Café. I finally asked her out! Do you remember the one? Tall, charcoal greyish hair, has a lot of piercings?"

"I know the one... but" I'm cut off.

"I'm thinking of taking her ice-skating that would be, literally, so *cool* wouldn't it..." He chuckles to himself.

"But Jack, I..." I try.

"Or perhaps bowling? Haven't been bowling in a while..."He continues.

"I really..." I try again.

"Nah, I don't really like bowling, maybe..."

"JACK!" I finally shout.

"What?!" He replies, looking slightly shocked, as if my tone just 'came out of nowhere', like he didn't deserve it.

"I can't cover you Wednesday" I finally say.

"What? Why not? This is really important to me you know!" He replies.

"I have a thing…" I can't help but look towards my letter, which I realise is just out on show for the world to see, I quickly stand up, practically sprint towards it and fold it over, pretending to straighten up a vase near it at the same time. As if having a wonky vase could require so much urgency. But he doesn't seem to notice.

He whines, "well can't you just cancel whatever 'thing' you have; this could be the start of the rest of my life!" He presses. He pulls out the 'puppy dog eyes' card, which would work on most other girls, but not me. I know what he's trying to do. I must stick to my guns!

"I'm sorry, I just can't. It's something I've already been putting off for way too long, and I really need to just do it". I feel a sense of pride in myself for being strong enough to say no. I'd love to help him out, and it is really unlike me not to; I hate letting people down. But sometimes I have to make myself a priority — another thing I picked up from therapy!

"Oh, that's disappointing, you were my only hope. Now I can't go. I felt sure she could've been 'The One' too, Lou, you know? The *ONE*". He stands up, his head hanging low and starts to walk out before I even have chance to take in what he just said.

"I'm sorry Jack, what am I thinking?" I don't know what I'm thinking... "Of course I'll do that for you, my thing wasn't that important anyway". And there it goes, just like that; my 'priority' status.

"Oh, thank you Lou, THANK YOU!" He jumps towards me with open arms and hugs me tightly, for what seems like forever. "How will I ever repay you?!" He finishes. But before I can even think about answering, he's galloped back towards and out of the front door in a bubble of happiness.

As I watch the front door close behind him I slump back down, peeking over with half an eye open and cringing with guilt at the folded letter on the side, I take a big gulp and think...Fuck, now what am I going to tell Sam?

Chapter Five

I bet Sam thinks I made the whole thing up, that there isn't even a letter to begin with. I thought I'd actually end up feeling relieved that I didn't have to go, and under some circumstances, I guess I would. But right now, the guilt is eating at me; I've let Sam down, when it should've been Jack. But the pain from Jack would've felt worse, and I don't want to be a bad friend. I look up towards my blank computer screen in an effort to control my sadness, but I'm too late, I feel a sting as tears start to cradle each eye and all I can think is the only one I've really hurt here is myself. My head slumps back down, my vision all blurred and I hear tiny drops of water starting to pat on to my lap.

So here I am, sat at my desk, at work, on my day off, covering Jack, crying my eyes out. They don't even *need* me; everything's already been done for the week. The orders have already been made and there are no deliveries until tomorrow, so there's no pressure today. I can't help but feel that I shouldn't be here at all.

I work at a jewellery factory in the city, nothing particularly special, but it pays the bills. Our company order and receive ring castings from suppliers (which is my job) and then, working through individual departments within the building, the rings are mounted, cut, set, lasered, polished, quality-controlled and finally shipped to fancy jewellery shops where they sell our products for about five-hundred percent more than the value price. It's daylight robbery, especially when you see some the sights of the people that work here. Here are a few of my juicy favourites;

So you've got Alex, a compulsive liar who pretends to be someone she's not. She makes up wild stories of this super-lavish lifestyle she lives, jet-setting every other weekend and having tea with the Queen, when in reality she just rents a flat above a shop and goes out once a week for fish and chips. I'd feel sorry for her, but she's really horrible towards Jack, my best friend. Jack does have a bit of a reputation though, he, let's say, has 'worked his way through' most of the office girls, but who can blame him, he's a handsome and very charming man in his early-20's. Before Jack knew any better, he and Alex used to date, but when he ended things she just couldn't get over it, so now she's just really bitter and makes sly comments about him whenever he's around.

You also have Julia who's the factory gossiper; she can't wait to get her beady eyes and ears in to someone else's business, mainly because her life is so pathetic and boring. She loves any drama, even fake drama, which she makes up sometimes to entertain herself if nothing else is really happening. She works in quality control, so she gets to see and speak to everyone; I guess this is how she gets her information!

Then there's Connie, who thinks she's 'too good' for this line of work and because she's worked here for a million years believes everyone else is below her. She manages to manipulate everyone else in to doing her job for her too, which I think is quite clever, but really, I just think everyone's terrified of her. I'm not entirely sure where Connie works, or is supposed to work; it's always been a bit of mystery.

Then there's Dan, who is the biggest brown-noser you've ever seen, he's like the boss' puppy, he follows her around begging for her affection twenty-four seven. He works all the hours under the sun for minimal wage, and then bitches about her behind her back for 'making him do it'. Dan works in polishing, but likes to think he's her number two. I don't know why he works so hard to try and impress her; she'll never want him in management.

And it's these sorts of people that are creating beautiful pieces of art every day. It's sad really that they have (well, apart from Connie, as someone else is doing her job) had *anything* to do with the making of it all.

I've been persuading the company to start doing bespoke items for years; I think there's a niche in the market for it. I'd love to be a buyer, or even a designer, that would be my dream job! But the boss, Katie, won't give my ideas the time of day; she's probably just too busy trying to direct those morons. She's nice though, as bosses go.

I've always had a love for art and design. I'm the sort of person that likes making presents for others, rather than buying. That's why before I proposed to Nicole two years ago I decided I would design the engagement ring that I would give to her. She has a specific taste and nothing I could find best suited her, so I thought, why not? I managed to acquire some 'computer-aided design' software from a friend in the business and it became my little side-project for those few weeks. I really enjoyed it and it turned out really well! That's what made me realise that I could actually *do* this.

The whole proposal actually went really well, too. I never imagined that I would be the one to do the proposing, I always dreamed that I would be the one that was proposed to. But I'd not long turned thirty and you can't stay young forever! I still wanted to look half-good in the wedding photos. And I'm pretty sure she was in no great rush, I'm not even sure it'd crossed her mind - she is a few years younger than me anyway!

On that perfect morning, the day she said yes to being my wife, we were exploring this fantastic lake, which was a mission in itself to get to. Winding steep, narrow roads with a mountain one side, and huge drop the other. It was the only day in spring that snowed, and my old car is definitely not made for bad weather or country driving at the best of times. I was pretty close at one point to stopping the car completely and proposing to her there and then, just in case the next bend were to bring death upon us. It was a realistic assumption that we may not have survived the journey to the lake and I was terrified, which helped mask the anxiety I already had from the anticipation of popping of the question at least. Even my monkey was still, in complete 'freeze' mode, for that trip. It was a close one. But we did manage to make it there safely and once we were there I was glad of my efforts, and the snow just made it even more magical. I heavily guarded my bag, which I entrusted to carry my creation as we walked the perimeter of the lake. She didn't seem too suspicious, which was good. I didn't have a speech prepared, or a 'moment' in mind. It was one of those times where you believe the most natural way is to 'go with the flow', but as a person that has a monkey in their head, this can be particularly difficult to do. I didn't have a choice though, because I had no idea what else to do. All my hopes were on the universe guiding me through it, by giving me a sign. And luckily, it did. Nicole, out of nowhere started this massive speech about how we're so lucky to have found each other, that she's the happiest she's ever been and finished with how we 'had to be together forever'. And that was the nudge I needed. I got on one knee, offered her the ring and repeated back to her that same last word; 'forever'?

She looked so surprised I thought she was going pass out! I'd never stood up so quick in my life! As I steadied her she nodded in affirmation and we both just started crying. It really was so perfect. We sat by that lake for hours after and I don't think she took her eyes off the ring the entire time.

Chapter Six

So, since I sent Sam an 'I have to cancel our appointment, sorry' text on Monday, she's tried calling me twice. Both times I 'accidently missed them', but in actual fact my phone ringing causes me a huge amount of panic - as we learnt before when I threw my phone in to the next room. I felt adult-enough to not do that today though when the second call came through. Instead, I handled it like a proper grown-up and... Ran away. Literally. I. ran.away. from.my.phone. And after a short conversation with myself after, my 'de-brief' of the incident, I in fact realised, that this was not a 'normal' reaction to that particular situation. Ways I could've handled it more effectively;

1. Accepted the call, like a normal person and had a normal conversation.
2. Touched 'decline' on the incoming call message and let it go to voicemail if I didn't want to have a conversation at that time.
3. Let it ring out, turn it on silent or power off completely until I was ready to have, said normal conversation.

4. Literally ANYTHING but let my monkey win. Fight and flight is definitely NOT necessary when it comes to answering a sodding telephone.

I eventually pluck up the courage to send her a text;

'Sorry I missed your calls, I was driving'. Lies. 'And sorry I had to cancel our last appointment too, something important came up, which I had to attend to. Louise.' Even more lies. But I think that one sounds more legitimate.

I instantly feel some relief now that I've not completely abandoned her. I'm back on track to fixing myself. I am winning again. Here I am - future-big-hero Lou!

Ten minutes pass and I've not had a reply yet. Oh my god, what if she's decided she doesn't want to work with me anymore, that I just waste her time, that I'm not worth bothering with? I know imagining this type of scenario isn't healthy, but I can't stop myself.
    I decide distraction is the best way to fend off these unhelpful thoughts. So I send a text to Jack;

'Hi mate, how did your date go yesterday? Fancy coming over? I have more gin!'

My phone beeps, a text straight back from Jack, good old reliable Jack; he doesn't hold me in suspense. He just drives me to drink in other ways!

'Hey Louey Pooey!' Ergh. I've never really liked that nickname, but I've also never said I didn't, so it's just carried on over the years, and I'm kind of stuck with it now. I guess it's affectionate though... In his own way. 'Sounds great, see you in half an hour?' I knew he couldn't refuse a boozy invite.

'Wonderful', I reply, 'see you then.'

Just as I'm about to set my phone down, thinking about what mixer to have, another text comes through. This time, it's from Sam.

'Hi Louise, that's not a problem, these things happen. Would you like to re-schedule? How about tomorrow? I've just had a slot free up at 11am? Sam.' I feel my palms getting sweaty again, and I haven't had any alcohol yet, so it can't be that this time. I finally put down my phone and take a deep breath. Why do I react this way to a text? It's *just* a text, I've got this. After my little prep talk, I manage a reply;

'That's great, I've penned you in. Thank you. Louise.'

Phew, I've done it. I can't believe it's only tomorrow though, that's not a lot of time. Not that I need to prepare or anything, but it's seems really damn close. Like, it's *tomorrow*. In only sixteen hours' time. S-i-x-t-e-e-n hours.

I can almost see my monkey rubbing its little hands together with delight, it's as if it's waiting on the side of a stage, the orchestra all set up ready for the signal. The spotlights are facing down and the curtains are coming up... No. No. *No*. Not going to happen. Your monkey tricks are *not* going to work on me. I will not perform for you! My head is swirling, I can't focus and my heart is beating so hard I can feel it in my throat. But then suddenly, there's a knock at the door, which brings me back to the room.

Jack! Thank the lord.

Chapter Seven

The thing I love most about Jack is his timing. And that he never (purposely) lets me down. Sometimes I feel like I don't treat him as well as I should, but it's not personal. Some days I just struggle to get by by myself. He doesn't know about my anxiety, I don't really feel anxious when he's around though, sometimes at work maybe? But the majority of the time, he just sees me as I really am, and I like that. That's why I'd never tell him about my monkey. I would hate for him to look at me weirdly, or treat me any differently. Like I'm this timid, fragile little bird that can't fend for herself. Because, believe it or not, without the anxiety, I'm a pretty fierce person too, I stand up for myself and what I believe in. Nicole thinks I'm brave, but how *can* I be if I'm afraid of nearly everything?!

"So how did the date go?" I ask as I hand him a very large glass of strawberry and watermelon gin, mixed with lemonade and crushed ice – my favourite!

"Yeah, it went okay ta, she's really nice. I think she must've felt quite comfortable with me too because we spoke about some pretty deep shit." He takes a swig from his glass and then immediately pulls a face. "Woah, how much gin did you put in this?"

"Oh, not a lot, I didn't think? Is it too much?" I wince back at him.

Jack, without hesitation replies; "never!" As if I just wildly offended him.

"So what sort of stuff did you talk about then?" I press.

"She told me that she gets like, social anxiety or something? She has panic attacks and everything! That's why she works at the café. Her shrink told her to push herself to be around others more, so she got that job, part-time, to work on her confidence. Pretty inspiring really, and interesting! She's not like anyone else I know." He continues on, but eventually his voice just blends in to the background. I'm no longer hearing anything he says. I'm shocked. Firstly, because he thinks he doesn't know anyone else like that, anyone with anxiety... And secondly, because, I honestly didn't think Jack had it in him to *understand* anything like that. I don't know why, and I feel guilty now for not giving him enough credit before. But I never felt like talking to him about my issues would be beneficial.

We continue on the rest of the evening getting more and more drunk, forgetting everything wrong with the world and just concentrating on having a great time. It's bliss.

***

I really must stop doing this drinking lark. This head-pounding is becoming all too familiar and all the more unwanted every time. I crack an eye open to scan my surroundings. I managed to make it to the bedroom this time, so that's an improvement. Passing out on the sofa, especially when you have company, can be seen as awfully rude.

I grab my phone, which is conveniently under my pillow and check the time. It's 11:45am and I have a missed call. From Sam. *Oh fuuuuuck*!

I jump out of bed, searching the room for clothing and as I do, the room spins and I have to sit back down again. "I can't believe I've done it again!" I share with the room. "Shiiit!"

I can't call her back, she might shout at me, or worse, be really disappointed. I'll just blame Jack again, he got me wasted, nothing to do with me not being responsible enough. "I'm so pissed off!" Somehow, by saying these things out loud, I feel like I'm giving myself a bollocking and therefore, no one else needs to. It's done now; I've learnt my lesson, let's all have a cup of tea (with an awful lot of sugars for this one) and move on. But unfortunately, life doesn't work like that.

Maybe I'll text her? No. That's not good enough... I know! I'll go in, yes, I'll go in! I'll go to the centre and explain to her that this is exactly the reason I need her to help me, because I'm obviously terrible at functioning by myself. I have no idea how I get though life without professional help!

I swear I never used to be like this, letting people down all the time, especially good ones that want to help me; it's like my number one rule of what NOT to do. Damnit!

Okay, so I have sufficient attire on, check, hair is tied up so I look a little less wild, check. No time to brush my teeth so I will pop a chewing gum in, yes good plan, check. I'm ready to go. As I run down the stairs in the most un-delicate way possible, I grab my letter and I shout to Jack, who's still lay comatose on the sofa "I'm just popping out, something I forgot to do!" I doubt that he'll hear it, but I say it anyway.

I get there at just past midday, not bad going, as wake-up calls go, but I'm too late. The centre closes early on a Friday. How did I not know that? So now, I'm back to square one. I *have* to call her.

Adrenaline's already pumping through my body from running for so long, so I might as well put it to good use. I bring up her name on my contact list and press 'call'. I put the phone to my ear and try to take back control my breathing before she answers. As I'm waiting for her to pick up, I realise that I feel a lot less anxious after exercise and if I don't over-think it, it doesn't affect me so much. This is like a minor breakthrough! I'm winning this one, monkey! Ha!

"Hello, this is Sam Vaughn, I can't get to the phone right now, but please leave your name and number and I'll get back to you as soon as possible. Thank you."

Argh, voicemail. Obviously I don't leave one. I still feel pleased with myself for trying though, that's the furthest I've come in a long time. I decide that I deserve a treat, so as I'm walking back home, I drop in to Anavrin Café for a Chai Latte; aka a hug in a mug. As I walk in the familiar warm, roasted coffee smell of the cafe hits me, for some reason it always makes me feel Christmassy. As I reach the till, a familiar face greets me, it's Emili, the woman Jack's been seeing! It occurred to me that I didn't actually know her name until now, after eyeing her name badge. I always imagined she would have a cool and edgy name, and I guess Emili, especially with the unusual spelling, is pretty cool! After taking my order, she asks my name for the cup, appearing oblivious to who I am, which initially confuses me, but I mean, how *would* she know I suppose? We haven't 'officially' met yet. After a long chain of thoughts before realising this, I eventually respond; "your future boyfriends bestest friend ever,

Louise!" Where the fuck did THAT come from? How awkward. This 'calling someone on the phone' lark has obviously done something strange to me.

"Oh, Louise! It's so nice to finally meet you!" She responds with a smile. Thank god, she doesn't think I'm some weirdo, or at least she doesn't let on that she does.

"Yeah, you too! I love this place", I respond quickly to move on, "you guys do the BEST Chai Latte's. Jack told me you guys were going out the other night, how did it go?"

"Yeah, it was amazing, thank you. He's such a good listener. We spoke about *everything*, it's like we've known each other forever! We're hoping to meet up again next week too." She grins.

I smile in return, not really knowing what else to say, and also not wanting to distract her too much whilst she's making my drink. It has to be made just right! But the unease starting to crease in her face tells me she may be feeling awkward with the silence between us.

"So, this might be a little forward of me to say", she starts, "but if you ever need someone to talk to about your anxieties, you can talk to me. I unfortunately know first-hand how difficult it can be to live with.

Someone once told me it was like having a monkey in your head, and I've never thought about it any other way since! Funny, but a pretty accurate metaphor I think!"

My mouth drops, not figuratively, but very much literally. Could she tell just by looking at me that I have anxiety too? But I feel okay right now, I dealt with the adrenaline and did a positive thing; I'm here treating myself because I thought I did so well. So what just happened?

"Sorry, I can see that probably wasn't the right thing to say. I mean..."

"No", I interrupt, "it's okay. It just took me by surprise I guess. How do you know that I... You know?"

"Well, when I was out with Jack the other night, I told him a lot about myself, maybe a little too much for a first date, but he told me that the things I was telling him sounded familiar to him, and he looked deep in-thought for a short while after. I asked him what he thinking about and he said you."

So, Jack, *knows*?! But how?! I've never let on to him, never once spoke to him about ANYTHING like that. Purposely. But maybe now, if he knows, and he hasn't looked at me weirdly or treated me any differently, that it's okay to talk to him? Oh, how did this happen? I'm so confused.

"Anyway, sorry, here's your drink, on the house and the offers there to chat, anytime okay?" I pick up my cup and notice her number written on the side. In a trance-like state I look up to her, thank her and walk out the door.

That was surreal. A million thoughts are running through my head, I feel in a daze, like I'm on auto-pilot walking home. I get just around the corner and notice my phone ringing. It's Sam. I can't do this *now*; the moment has well and truly long passed. I turn my phone off, get home, walk straight past a still very comatose Jack and get back in to bed. It's still warm. And pink bears there. I stroke his, not-really-very-pink-anymore-it's-been-loved-too-much fur and gently soothe myself to sleep.

It's a dream, all a dream.

Chapter Eight

Except it isn't. I stay upstairs for as long as I can in hope that Jack will wake up, not want to disturb me, and leave quietly. But I really need the loo now and there's only one and it's downstairs, argh! My monkey is chuckling away, dancing from side to side and banging at its hypothetical tambourine. Yes, it has a tambourine sometimes. Mainly when it's especially pleased, imagine that. I manage to wait another hour and half before I can't take it any longer. I NEED to go. The desperate state of my bladder has out-weighed any panic about the very real likelihood of bumping in to Jack. I tip-toe as best I can, my thighs moulded together tightly to prevent any potential leakage. No-one wants that. As I turn the corner on the stairs I notice a vacant sofa where a Jack-shaped person used to be and I peer around the room cautiously. Thankfully, the coast is clear. I run as fast as I can to the toilet and. Ah, relief. I sit there for a few minutes after just to completely appreciate how much better I feel.

As I make my way back through the living room, I see a note on the side. It's from Jack;

'Afternoon sleepyhead! Thanks for a cracking night! See you Monday, lots of love xxx'.

Phew. Panic over. It's times like these that I especially miss Nicole. She would know exactly what to do and say in this sort of situation. She's my rock. I'm so lucky to have her. But with her being away I feel quite alone. And it's not like I can just pick up the phone, which I normally *would* be able to do with her, because right now, she's out in the middle of a signal-free jungle. Typical, the one person that I *can* phone, *can't* answer. She said it's a 28-day expedition, and I know we're only in to the second week. But SO much has already happened already in that time.

I just miss her.

Chapter Nine

It's the weekend now, but my weekend to work. It makes no sense that I have to work weekends. It just seems so unnecessary! Jack and I work on alternate weekends so at least I won't have to face him just yet. I have no idea what I'm going to say to him when I do see him, but I'll have to think of something. He'll already know that Emili and I have spoken; she would've no doubt given him a 'heads-up'. As I imagine how that scenario goes, I get rudely interrupted;

"Before you do your next order Monday, I need you to do a stock take of what we already have. I'm putting you in charge of this, as I'm taking the rest of the weekend off. It's essential this is done by Monday, Louise, we cannot afford to get behind this month". And just like a viper attack, she comes, she bites, she goes. I barely had a chance to open my mouth. If I'd have blinked, I think I'd have missed her. I let out a sigh. Just like that, my quiet weekend is well and truly over. I had planned to sit and stew on what I would say to Jack when I next see him, but I have no time for that now! Katie is such a bitch. I've changed my mind about her. Why did I ever think she was 'nice'? Bollocks to her and her viper bites.

I'm going to need some help with this so I decide to contact admin, who also, oversee the safes. Because you know, it makes complete sense that hundreds of thousands of pounds worth of gold, diamonds and other precious metals and stones aren't heavily guarded from some top security firm, but by admin. I wonder if they're paid more than minimum wage. Anyway, I pick up the phone and dial their number. Alex answers.

"Hi Alex, it's Lou from upstairs. I need your help to do some stocktaking with me. Katie left it with me to organise. I think it'll pretty much take up our weekend though, sorry."

"Argh Louise, I was *just* getting in to my crossword!" She's obviously super busy today too...

"Okay, fine!" She whines in a perfect teenage-esque tone. That was easier than I was expecting though.

I grab a quick brew and head downstairs. I love tea. Tea makes me happy. It's my go-to drink; it always makes me feel better. Feeling un-motivated? Cup of tea. Feeling un-inspired? Cup of tea. Feeling... Pretty much anything really? Cup of tea! It's a habit that's been handed down to me from my Mom, Elizabeth, or

LAUREN FRENCH

Ellie, as she likes to be called. She used to make me tea all the time, so, naturally, it reminds me of home and feeling safe and content. My Dad, Fredrick, or Fred, as *he* likes to be called, hates tea and is very much a coffee drinker, but I never really get on with the stuff (which loosely translates as 'it makes me shit a lot'), so I just stick to tea. And black tea at that, as it's healthier. I try and avoid sugar too, unless I'm feeling sorry for myself in anyway. By this, I mean if I'm ever;

1. Sad
2. Hung-over
3. Ill
4. Over-tired
5. Struggling with life in general

Which, come to think of it, is a lot of the time! If I ever drink tea without sugar, you know that I'm having a pretty okay time! Today though, I'm having sugar.

"So I heard that *Jack* is seeing some new woman now?" Alex spits at me. And I realise now why she didn't put up much of a fight about helping me out. She wants information...

"Alex, I'd rather not discuss Jack with you," I start, all professional, "I don't want to upset you or anything if you still..."

"What?" She cuts me short. "If I still what? Love him? Ha! Are you kidding? Not me, *no*, I've moved on. In fact, I moved on a LONG time ago". Hmm yeah. Certainly sounds like it.

Julia suddenly appears, as if her sixth sense has spiked and there's some free gossip she ought to know. I was half-expecting it to be honest. "Have you come to help Julia?" I quiz.

"Erm, no. Just thought I'd see who was down here, you know. These safes aren't guarded as well as they should be! I was concerned!" And with that, she disappeared as quickly as she appeared. I have a feeling she's not gone too far away though. Sad cow.

"So as I was saying". Alex, completely ignoring Julia's entrance (and swift exit) attempts to dig a little more. "I just thought I'd ask how he was doing is all, you know, I haven't seen him in a while."

"Well", I reply, "he's doing alright thank you. Seems his normal, happy self." She looks away, her face almost charred by my comment. I try to move on as quick as I can, but on the spot I can't think of anything to say, I know we can't talk about Jack anymore and she'll only continue to try to, so, what to say... What to say... Ah, I've got it! "Lovely weather we've been having isn't it?" Sweet Jesus, Lou, good work, she won't suspect a thing.

Our small talk continues like this for the rest of the afternoon. But we manage to plough through two of the three safes, so I'm pleased with that. Just the last one to do tomorrow and I'll be ready for Monday. Look at me, all boss-like, getting shit done. Maybe if I can prove to Katie how good a job I can do she'll consider listening to my ideas.

***

Monday is here and I STILL haven't figured out what I'm going to say to Jack. Maybe I'll keep it casual like; 'hey Jack, how's your hangover hanging?' Because he's bound to have one. And then move in with a subtle 'So, you know your girl Emili... she said you were thinking about me?' Oh god no, that sounds awful, and very much NOT like me. I can't expect him to treat me 'normally' if I don't act 'normal' towards him. I try again. 'Hi Jack, look, Emili told me that you think I have anxiety, well, you're sooo wrong, stop making shit up about me to someone you barely know.' Oh wow, really not right. I feel like this is a game of goldilocks porridge. First bowl was too hot, the next too cold, I need to think of something that's 'just right'. Okay. I've got it this time. 'Hey Jack, how're you? How was your weekend?' The door slams and I sit up straight, and a little bit of wee comes out. I really need do something about my pelvic floor. Maybe my friends were right, I am getting old.

"Hey LoueyPooey!" Jack greets me with a huge smile. He looks okay considering how hung-over he must be. I can still smell the booze on him as he leans in for a hug. Knew it.

"Hi Jack", I wince, "how're you? How was your weekend?" Yes! So far so good.

"Yeah it was great thanks, had breakfast with Emili yesterday, you are going to LOVE her when you meet her properly, she's so smart and so funny! She's an all-rounder". I can almost see him swooning as he stares out the window next to me. I wonder if that means she hasn't said anything to him? 'When I meet her properly... he knows we've met. Oh my god. I'm definitely over-thinking this. I decide to try and go against all my rules and simply 'go with the flow' with this one, usually works out okay.

We chat back and forth all for a short while, like nothing's happened and everything seems normal. I really was just over-thinking it, wasn't I? See? Everything's fine. And breathe.

I'm glad Jack's here and cheering me up, even if he doesn't know he is. This morning was so shit, I got all that stocktaking done, managing NOT to kill Alex in the process, and yet Katie barely acknowledged it. I'm really not sure why I expected anything more. Just as I decide to let myself relax completely in Jack's company he starts to say exactly what I didn't want him to say.

"So Emili told me you guys had a nice chat the other day?" I nearly fall over, even though I'm sat down. I start to scratch at the back of my neck, which I tend to do when I feel on the spot and like I can't escape. I'm hot. It's almost as if someone's just shoved a radiator under my blouse and turned the heat up full blast.

"Erm... Oh yeah I did! I'd completely forgotten about that! How bizarre!" I lie. My foot starts tapping on the floor involuntarily. *Why* is he bringing this up?!

"Look", he starts. Oh god, I can feel myself seriously over-heating. I feel like I'm actually panting. "We don't have to talk about anything you feel uncomfortable with, but just so you know, I'm here for you anytime, okay?" He must be able to sense my discomfort. "You don't need to say anything, let's just get on with our work." He smiles and turns around and faces his desk behind me.

I manage a nod, but not sure if he caught it before turning around. Right now, I have tambourine cymbals still ringing in my ears but I feel kind of relieved. I'm glad he knows. I am. I feel like a weight's been lifted somehow. I have someone I can talk to now if I need to. Which in retrospect, I guess I do. I still haven't moved any further forward with Sam. Maybe I can do something really out-of-the-ordinary and ask *Jack* for a favour this time...

"Actually, Jack", I hesitate, but carry on pushing through, despite the cymbals getting louder. "I do want to ask a favour of you". He turns to me on his swivel chair.

"Of course, what is it?" He asks, optimistically.

"Could you call my shrink, Sam, on my behalf and organise another appointment for me please? I'm free tomorrow, Thursday and Friday next week. Any of those are good." I respond, in lightning speed. Any hesitation and I may stutter.

He looks shocked. Oh no. I shouldn't have said anything, what was I thinking?! "Lou, I had no idea you were seeing a shrink?" I can hear the empathy in his voice, but I still want to escape.

"Oh it's okay, I'm okay." I try to sound more upbeat, as I still don't want him to think I'm a timid and fragile little bird. "But I've missed two appointments with her now". Both kind of your fault, I'm thinking. But in all honesty, I know it's all mine. "And I'm afraid of calling her to try again in case she gets angry or upset with me for wasting her time or something." Wow I don't think I took a breath that entire time, I suddenly realise.

"Of course I'll do that for you! It's the very least I can do." He soothes. I can tell he feels taken aback, but he seems okay with it nonetheless. And I'm relieved. He does owe me a favour or two, after all.

I'm exhausted! What a rollercoaster. I just want to go home and sleep now, but I can't. I still have four more excruciating hours at work left. I hope Jack doesn't try and talk to me anymore about it, I don't think I could cope.

Dan taps on our office door and comes straight in, without looking at anyone, his eyes fully focussed on a clipboard that he's carrying. Why does he need a clipboard to polish rings? I can't help but wonder.

"Katie wants me to go round asking everyone for 'suggestions'. She has a meeting with the head honchos later this week and wants to take some ideas forward. So do either of you have any? He asks with sass.

"Well, actually", I start, "I have tried to talk to her before about an idea I had." I wait for him to look at me before I continue. Rude bastard. He finally drags his eyes off his clipboard to look at me. It's like his eyes must weigh a tonne. What an effort.

"Well?" He asks, impatiently.

"I think we should start doing bespoke jewellery! Designing, making and even selling items ourselves. It's a no-brainer; cut out the middle-man and sell straight to the customer. We could all work from home and do it online - saves on rent too!" I respond excitedly, thinking out loud.

"Ermmmmm... No. Terrible idea. Do *you* have anything Jack?" He shifts his gaze to Jack, who has been trying to avoid Dan's question (and existence, probably), this entire time.

Before Jack can even open his mouth, I start yelling at Dan before I can persuade myself to stop -"Wait, *what?!* What's wrong with that? I think it could really work!" How dare he just dismiss me like that!

"I think Lou's idea's pretty inspiring to be fair Dan". Jack chimes in. Cheers mate.

"Hmm, yes well, as I already said, that one's ruled out. Okay, thanks anyway." And with that, Dan swivels back on his heel and shuts the door abruptly back behind him. I can think of something else he could also go and swivel on.

"Who the fuck does he think he is?!" I can't help projecting to the room. I look to Jack, who's now half looking away; a fearful look to his face.

"As if any of those fuckers would have any ideas half as good as that? He makes me so mad, the disrespectful bastard!" I continue, gesturing to the door, as if he's there, still stood in front of it.

Jack, looking around the room for sudden inspiration replies; "I'm sorry Dan was a dick to you just then, Lou, but you know what he's like. You shouldn't be surprised by him." I glare at him. He looks even more scared now.

"Erm. Anyway, Lou!" He tries again, continuously reviewing the situation as he goes along. "As I was saying, this phone call you want me to make."

"Ah yes" and I'm back in the room. And the anger magically transforms back in to fear.

"Leave me the details before you go and I'll sort that out for you later." He tries a smile, unsure of whether it's safe to yet or not.

"Thanks, Jack, I really appreciate it." I finally say, and try a smile back.

Chapter Ten

Well, thanks to Jack, I've managed to get another appointment with Sam. And here I am now; stood outside the Saxony Health Centre plucking up as much courage I can just to walk in. Jack did ask if I wanted him to come with me, but I said no, because I felt already embarrassed enough about the whole thing. He's been really good to me since though, and no 'acting weirdly' either, which I'm grateful for.

I haven't been to the centre for about a year now. And I can't say I'm pleased to be back, even if it is just a one-off appointment. I had this dream that I'd be able to walk out of that door for the last time and never look back. That I would be cured and my life would be back to normal again! But come to think of it, I don't think my life has ever been 'normal'.

I feel like I can't put it off much longer, I'm here, but I'm still really early, twenty minutes early to be precise! I do this all the time, well, when I remember that I have appointments anyway! I can't stand the thought of being late. It's an added stress that I really don't need, but it doesn't particularly help me by going in really early either because when I do arrive I'm just sat around waiting, and waiting's the worst. Time slows down and thoughts get louder and wilder. It's a horrible combination. Hours before an appointment, I'm just clock-watching, building up more and more worry and stress with each passing minute. It's a living nightmare.

As I walk towards the building I realise it looks exactly the same. Really old, dreary and still absolutely terrifying. Oh, I'm not sure I can do this. My stomach does an almighty lurch and I feel instantly nauseous. I try my best to calm my pulse and steady my pace, but with every beat it seems to power more churns and I can't stop it. I coil over and grab my stomach, trying my best to walk towards the small, adjacent wall to the side of the building where normally I sit before an appointment to build up some courage, I just manage to put a hand on to the familiar, crumbling brick to steady myself and... BLEURGH. Oh no, this is *so* not good. The courage-wall is covered in my vomit - that's not a great start! Fuck! What am I going to do? My head is spinning and I just can't focus. Why can't I focus! My monkey is screaming with glee, bashing away at its tiny tambourine. I wipe my mouth with my sleeve and take my jacket off. I head back to the car, where I know I have chewing gum. I can still fix this, it will NOT win! The cymbals get quieter and I make an attempt at some grounding techniques. I pop a chewing gum in and try to find five red-coloured things. Okay let's go;

1. My car.
2. That signpost across the car park.
3. That woman's shoes.
4. The pen on my dashboard.
5. Part of the rainbow that's in the centres window.

Okay, good. Now five things that I can hear;

1. The wind in the trees.
2. A bird singing.
3. A car driving past.
4. The beeping of the ticket machine.
5. Not those *stupid* cymbals. Thank god. I think it's working.

I take in some deep breaths and steady myself. I look at the time and decide it's now or never.

Chapter Eleven

As I enter, I'm greeted by a familiar face, the receptionist, Heather. She takes my name and offers me a seat in the waiting room. The dreaded, fear-invoking waiting room. Before I let myself fall in to old tricks, I continue with some more self-help techniques that Sam taught me. I brought with me a stone, sounds crazy but, Nicole found me this stone, she gave it to me because she thought it was pretty. And it is! She's so romantic. I was told once that penguins do a similar thing, they go out searching endlessly for the 'perfect pebble', and once they find it, they offer it to their love. If it's accepted, they're then together forever. It's such a simple and beautiful gesture.

I take the stone out my pocket and look at in closely, taking in its every detail. Once I've done this, I close my eyes and feel all its different textures and grooves. I'm giving my full concentration and all of my senses to it and I start to feel calm.

"Mrs Louise Grainger?" I hear. I suddenly jump out of my trance.

"Yes, here!" I say dutifully.

And here we go.

"It's been a long time, Louise! How have you been?" Sam starts, ushering me towards a chair in her office. It has a beautiful oak wood, four-legged frame with lime green cushioning. Reminds me a bit of my rocking chair at home, where I wish I was right now. I take the seat and a deep breath in, for good measure.

"Mostly okay, I think. But more recently I've been finding it hard to control my monkey". If I gave that response to literally anyone else in the world (well, maybe apart from Emili), it would made absolutely no sense at all, but Sam gets it.

"Okay, that's fine; we can work together on that." I instantly feel more settled, my monkey however, perks up at the potential risk. "Has anything changed in your life that you can think of perhaps more recently that may have led you to feel like this now?" She prods.

I sit and ponder for a moment before responding with; "maybe it's because my wife's away at the moment. She's been travelling the last three weeks and I've had a lot of alone time which I've struggled with I guess. I thought it'd be fun initially, you know, doing whatever I want to do, when I want to do it, but it turns out I feel quite lonely and I can't really contact her because there's no signal in the jungle." As I say it I surprise myself. I didn't realise I'd felt like this.

"That would make complete sense; of course it must be hard for you, to be anxious about her being away, and especially with not being able to contact her. An increased level of anxiety is actually a normal response to that situation. Remember our chart?" She continues.

"Yeah, I think so", I try. She drew me this like reaction 'thermometer' on her whiteboard last year with different levels on it. I was given a range of scenarios and I had to answer each one with where I think I *my* level of anxiety would be on it. Then I'd have to answer the same scenarios again with what level I thought a 'normal level of response' would be. Then we discussed how to better manage my emotions in order to normalise my reactions. It was all really interesting and it made a lot of sense at the time, but I'm not so sure now. My temperature feels off the thermometer completely.

"Remember, regulating your emotions takes practice. And don't forget, sometimes what we believe isn't always the truth. When faced with something you're unsure of, ask yourself, 'is this a fact or is it a belief?' Before you build your anxieties up to a state you can't control, rein that monkey in." Imagining it on a leash makes me feel instantly better. Ha! I'm sorry I ever doubted you Sam, you do deserve every penny I'm paying you - you do have all the answers! And now I have the tools and the know-how, monkey. It's all coming back to me. I'm so glad I did this, I needed it. I needed to remember.

After a while, Sam finally asks me how I felt about writing my letter and I don't answer straight away. I take it out of my pocket, un-fold it and look down at my scribbles. "They're just words, the *right* words", I say, "but not ones I really *feel*. So in answer to your question, Sam, I don't really feel anything about it." I know that if I did feel anything that I probably wouldn't be here, but saying it out loud makes me realise it I suppose. "Well, actually, it does make me kind of sad. But only because I wish I could go back in time and change things."

"Do you mind if I take a look?" Sam suggests. I hand her the paper in hope she spots something I hadn't. We both sit in silence for a few minutes whilst she works through it.

"This is a good, Louise." Sam announces. "It looks like you understood the task really well and it reads beautifully."

"Sounds like something out of a movie" I joke. But really, I'm wondering whether maybe I *do* know, and it is there after all, somewhere inside me, the answer to it all. *The cure!*

"No, this is more *real* than a movie, Louise. You've captured something special in here." I'm hoping the 'something special' isn't the words underneath my crossings out!

"Then why can't *I* see it?" I ask desperately. I hear the frustration in my voice, so she must have.

"My suggestion is, read it again, and again out-loud, and then maybe again to a family member, or a friend. It could be that you need to say it out-loud or to an audience for you to really *feel* it."

***

Overall, I found it really useful, but the last part seemed rather pointless. Read it again? Like I haven't already tried that. Out loud? I'd sound like a right moron! And to a family member or friend? Are you having a laugh? Because if you're not, then *they* definitely will. What a joke. That's never going to happen. NEVER.

Chapter Twelve

Anxiety has very much become a part of my life. Feeling anxious is the 'norm' now. If I don't feel anxious, something's wrong. How crazy does that sound? But it's true, strangely. I can't seem to be able to simply rest like normal people do. I find it ironic, that days off work are called 'rest days'; I have no idea how to do that. Even when I try to force myself to rest (which defeats the object doesn't it really) I can't. I put a movie on and try to absorb myself in to it, in an attempt to lure myself in to a state of peace. But no chance. I don't even realise it, but I'm told I still sit there fidgeting; my subconscious mind unsettled. Anxiety is a bad habit. Because I've had it for as long as I can remember, it *has* become my norm. How do you even begin to change the habit of a lifetime? 'Practising positive language' and 'challenging my negative thoughts' is hard. And exhausting! It's an addiction I never deserved. A fight I never instigated. It's just *so* unfair.

My phone starts buzzing in my pocket and I gasp in horror. Oh no, not again. I can't do this, I really can't. I pull it out and see Nicole's name. No way, it can't be?

Is it really? Oh my god, *oh my god*, I feel a wave of excitement rush over me and again it rushing back down as I realise something might be wrong. I answer tentatively. "Hello? Nicole?"

"Hey you! How're you doing? I thought I'd give you a surprise call as we've reached our next camp and it has signal, finally! I've missed you so much!" She talks at a million miles per second, as if she could lose that precious signal again at any time and wants to get everything in all at once!

"Oh my god, Nicole!" I cry. "I've missed you so much too!" Tears start to fall immediately, it's only been three weeks, but it feels like *years*.

"Aww my love, don't cry! I'm having the best time! But I wish you were here with me, I've seen so many amazing things!" She gleams. I can't help but feel guilty about telling her how I've actually been feeling this last few weeks; so instead, I decide to tell her a little white lie.

"Yeah, and everything's great here!" I move on sharply, "I can't wait to hear all about your trip!"

"Only another week to go and I'll be home. Are you still okay to pick me up?" She confirms.

"Absolutely! I'll be there at the 'arrivals' hall with one of those handmade signs '*Nicole Grainger*'" I put

on a posh voice and snort. She laughs. Good. The coast
is clear. She doesn't suspect a thing.

"Make sure you take lots of photos! I want know
every detail of your trip when you get back." I continue.

"Oh I will!" She promises. "My favourites are the
monkeys, they're absolutely hilarious! I have loads of
photos of them. There are sooo many different types!
But my favourites are the howlers. They're so noisy
and their 'howls' just sound like huge, long burps, it's
so funny!"

"Sounds brilliant!" I reply. I'm so pleased for her.

"And this one monkey," she continues, "we left
some trail mix for, and it was crazy Lou, we watched it
swing down from this huge tree to collect it, we
couldn't believe it, it came sooo close to us!" I smile as
I sit and realise that I don't need to go to the jungle to
be able to interact with monkeys, although it would
be nice to see them in their own, natural habitat
sometime. I imagine my monkey burping along to its
tambourine and this makes me laugh-out-loud.

We talk for a little while longer and I tell her about
Jack and his new girlfriend as they're all cute and
'official' now! He was so excited to tell me, so much so
it looked like he was going to cry, which isn't like Jack
at all; he must really like this one. I also tell her about

my bitch boss and all the extra work I've had to do with no thanks. And how much I hate Dan for being so rude to me. Trivial stuff really compared to her current life, but she still wants to hear about my things, which is nice. She then asks if I've seen or spoken to any of my family since she'd been gone and I admitted that I hadn't, I didn't even realise I hadn't until she asked. I decide that I would make every effort to contact them for a catch-up soon.

"Well, I'd best go" she finishes. "It's my turn to cook tonight and I haven't got anything prepared yet! It won't be long until we're together again, Louise. I love you so much."

Her words resonate with me the rest of the day and I feel so much better, hopeful, safe. It's like I'm in a trance. A love trance. She's my escape from all the shit in the world. It won't be long, we really *will* be together again, very soon. And breathe.

Chapter Thirteen

I can't stop smiling. It was so good to hear her voice! To think she's over five-thousand miles away in the Amazon and I was able to just speak to her. It's remarkable!

In the hype, I type a quick message to the 'Grainger Family' group chat to see how everyone's doing. We arrange to meet up for a barbeque at the weekend. That'll fill up my 'rest' days with something to look forward to!

I've really missed seeing my Mom and Dad. They've been busy recently with re-decorating the house, which I tell myself, is the reason that I've not been in-touch as much. They have an empty nest now that my not-so-little-he's-a-lot-taller-than-me-now younger brother, Rob moved out this year and they're both now retired. I think that's why they've re-decorated; for a brand new start. Rob and I used to get up to all sorts of mischief, we never really grew up. Our favourite past-time was ruthlessly abusing our poor mother's fear of spiders. We'd spend hours at a time scheming our next trick. My favourite memory, which I cherish closest, is the time we got her with a 'spider' hairball. Let me explain. Every now and then I'd pull all the hairs off my hairbrush, roll them up in to a ball and just throw them away. But on this particular day, my brother, watching on thoughtfully, decided we could use the hairball to scare our poor mother. So together, we devised a cunning plan until it was time to do the deed. We fought back our laughter as we both yelled from my bedroom in the familiar *'help-us-we're-going-to-die'* call to our unsuspecting mother, the tone she knew as 'there's a spider present that needs urgent removal'. She hated them, but she was the brave one. So she came hurtling up the stairs in a heroic bid to save us from this unwelcome beast, and as she entered the room I turned on my hairdryer, aimed at the ball, which made it fly across the bedroom floor, bounding towards her feet at speed. She shrieked in the highest pitch known to humankind and ran back down the stairs in absolute terror. It was the prank of our lives.

Makes sense now that Robs a mechanic, as he really did *drive* everyone mad. Our poor parents had so much patience. We're so lucky to have them. It's a shame that, since I moved out four years ago to live with Nicole, Rob and I became more distant. I know that people can drift, and it's normal when you have your own lives to live, but I still regret it. I could've tried harder. But he seems okay, and he now lives with his fiancée, Jenny, who's really lovely. She's his penguin.

They've asked me to bring a pudding to the barbeque, as they love my baking. But I haven't baked anything since I nearly killed my sister in-law, Dee. For some reason it slipped my mind that she's allergic to nuts and I decided to use almonds in my family-famous apple flan, which I *never* do. I only used them because Nicole hadn't been eating them and they needed to be used up. I don't even like them! I felt truly awful though and I've never forgiven myself for it, so much so I haven't baked since. Her poor husband Owen, Nicole's brother, was mortified, as was Nicole. I think her parents felt weirdly relieved though because her Mum, Sharon had done it, also accidently I might add, two years previously. I bet Dee dreads coming over now. I think I'll buy a pudding for the weekend and pass it off as my own, for everyone's safety.

Whilst we're on the subject of my in-laws, I have to say, I drew a great bunch. Nicole's Mum and Dad, Sharon and Ron have always treated me like one of their own. They're wonderful people with hearts of gold. It was actually Sharon that got me in to baking! My folks rarely did anything like that, but Sharon showed me how. It's an art in itself. I really enjoy it, or at least I really used to!

Chapter Fourteen

How is it Monday morning again? They always seem to come around so fast! It doesn't help when I overhear Connie's pitchy voice talking over everyone else's in the break room either.

"Yeah, the meeting went well apparently. She got a load of ideas. But there was one in particular that stood out from the rest, and the guys at the top said it was 'one worth investing in'." She squeals excitedly. "I know it's mine, it's *got* to be."

I turn to Jack, who has just joined me, and I can't help but notice how refreshingly healthy he looks for a Monday morning. I realise I have to take the opportunity to say so. "Bloody hell Jack, you don't look shit-awful for a change today!" I have a way with words.

"Erm, yeah. Cheers, mate!" He replies in a sarcastic, yet positive tone. "Emili has decided we need to be healthier, so one of my things is to cut out booze for the few weeks, see what happens." He shrugs.

"Wow, really? Fair enough!" This surprises me more than the 'idea' thing, which I was planning on talking to him about before I noticed the warm glow in his face.

"Anyway," I continue, the idea thing - "do you really think Connie's idea is worth investing in?"

"Doubt it; it's only to get a better coffee machine and comfier chairs. Seems pointless really." He responds carelessly.

"Yeah that doesn't sound very ground-breaking." I conclude.

We grab our freshly made brews, which I might add, are fine as they are, and drag ourselves back to our little office. We sit there setting our desks up for a few minutes, gathering paperwork and making sure the radio is set to our favourite station (important stuff), not that it should've changed, but sometimes Dan likes to fuck about with it to piss us off.
Speak of the devil, here he comes - *'the whirlwind of fume'* – our nick-name for Dan because every time we see him, we end up fuming.

"Morning guys! How was your weekend? Jack, I know you were here, but you probably haven't heard the big news yet!" His smile is spread ear-to-ear, his knees are bending inwards, looking like he's trying to hold a wee in out of excitement; he can barely contain himself. I think he'll explode. My thoughts are rudely interrupted by his sudden burst of verbal diarrhoea.

"MY IDEA WON! I'M GOING UP WOOHOO!" He proclaims, dancing on the spot and pointing his index fingers in the air. He eyes us both, dying for one of us to ask him about it. Even though neither of us *want* to know, we'll *have* to ask else he'll never leave. Jack also realises this and beats me to it;

"You're going up where, Dan?" He asks, rolling his eyes.

"To management!" He replies, abruptly, "I've finally got it! All it took was one little idea and here I am! I am SO excited! I've worked so hard for this. And after all this time!" He's in his own little dream-world now; ergh, I don't think he'll ever leave our office. I make a discerning face towards Jack, which obviously Dan spots and he suddenly becomes still. Oh my god. I have secret powers. He frowns at me, but then his face twists in to some sort of psychotic grin and I suddenly feel terrified; I have become the prey. My monkey has taken this opportunity and is now running with it. It feels attacked. To be fair, I also feel attacked. So it's actually doing its job properly for once! Well this is one good thing, I think to myself, imagining that they're probably going to be my last thoughts.

"Well, Louise." He pulls in closer to me, close enough for me to be able to smell his cheap aftershave, probably one he got from his great-aunt for Christmas. "Sometimes you have to *shit* on people to get what you want in this place." He spits. "And unfortunately for you, *you* were the one that was shat on this time." He pulls away, but for a moment all I can think is that I already *knew* I'd been shat on by the stench coming from his neck. Yuck! I think nothing more of it, only grateful for his retreat and he leaves. For some reason, I'm panting hard and I feel like bursting in to tears, that was a close call, but I didn't die. I'm safe. I see Jack get off his seat out the corner of my now wet eye and follow him out. He looks like he's on a mission.

He soon arrives back at the other side of the door, but doesn't open it. I can see his eyes though, through the slits in the blind. He looks in a state of shock, but somewhere behind it is fire. He looks like he's trying to calm himself down. He finally opens the door and I nearly spill my tea.

"Jack, are you okay?" I ask, putting my cup down. This is serious.

"That scumbag weasel. I went out there to confront him and tell him to back the fuck away from you, which I did, but..." He stops.

"What happened, Jack?" I wait. Nothing. "Please, tell me? What is it?" My voice breaks. I can feel my heart racing again. What the hell is going on?!

"It's Dan, he..." He pauses again. "He...*Stole* your idea." He practically whispers.

"He... WHAT?!" I shout. The contrast in our volumes is colossal.

"I'm sorry, Lou, that's what he just told me, that's all I know, I..." He tries. But I'm no longer listening. My thoughts are pulsing around my head at nanospeed, shooting from one side to another in flashes. I can't seem to grab on to one single thought, they're all moving too fast. So I just shout in an attempt to get their attention.

"ARGH!" I finally let out. "I'm going to get that little SHIT!" And as I stand up, I have that same fire that Jack had in him, only his seems to have died down.

"Wait!" Jack shouts, grabbing my arm. "I'm sorry Lou, but think about this. Going in and having it out with him, or anyone else for that matter like this won't be helpful." He suggests.

"I don't care Jack, I'm livid! Who does he think he is! He shouldn't be allowed to get away with this!" I argue.

I'm so hurt and this is so unfair. I exhale exhaustedly and crash back in to my chair.

"No, you're right" he agrees. "He shouldn't, and he won't. Let's think about this practically."

Jack has a plan. He tells me he's going to go and see Katie over lunch, so not to interrupt our productivity during work time (not that there's going to be much of that anyway this morning), and discuss what actually happened when Dan was asking for ideas last week.

I clock-watch all morning, willing its hands to rebel and just tick a little faster. But I think the clock is actually beginning to conspire against me, time has stood still and 'lunch-time' is just a concept, an unreachable myth.

But, by some miracle, it does arrive and the deed is done. The truth is out. I couldn't face that conversation myself, even as a fly on the wall (or an ear pressed against the other side of the door), so Jack went alone. He's my hero; I will never be able to re-pay him for this. It's amazing what you can see through the slits in our office door blind though, I saw Kate going in, Jack going in, Jack coming out, Dan going in, Dan coming out, then Katie coming out. She followed Dan all the way down the stairs and out of sight. Jack opens our office door and practically puts my head through the window in it, I didn't realise he was coming and he knocked me flying.

"Oh shit, Lou, sorry, are you okay?" He sympathises.

"It's no bother, what happened?!" I pry.

"Got the fucker sacked didn't I? For gross misconduct! It's basically fraud!" He glows, even brighter than before.

"Oh my god Jack, are you serious?" I respond, feeling immediately guilty and worried.

"Don't do that, Lou, whatever it is you're doing to yourself", noticing my face change. "He deserved everything he got!"

I nod in agreement, amazed at how observant Jack really is. He's the best. "Thank you so much, Jack." I eventually manage.

Wow, that was incredible. And easily the single-most exciting thing that's literally EVER happened in this god-awful factory. Someone getting marched off the premises! Whoa!

We decide that we need to celebrate that evening, even though Jack swore not to drink, it would be illegal not to right now. What a win! Finally that little rat is gone, no more whirlwinds of fume!

Chapter Fifteen

I arrive at my Mom and Dad's that weekend, complete with fancy pudding. M&S's Finest Sicilian Lemon Cheesecake. I had to choose a good one if they 'love' my baking; they're going to think I've really out-done myself this time! Which I have in a way, I had to go out specifically to pick it up and I paid a small fortune for it too, they're not cheap, you know!

"Hello!" I yell, letting myself in and throwing my keys on the side – my normal coming home routine. I nearly forget to put the pudding down before Charlie jumps all over at me with excitement, but luckily I remember just in time, phew. What a greeting though! Charlie is a very hyper Springer Spaniel; springing's in their name and nature! He's so lovely though, makes me want my own, but Nicole's not keen. Likes monkeys, dislikes dogs, what's that all about?!

"Ah, you made it! And with pudding I see!" I giggle to myself imagining that Nicole's with me, getting called pudding. I make a mental note of that and decide that will be my new nickname for her when she returns.

"Of course!" I reply.

I walk through the house, making sure to point out everything new that I see, knowing full well that if I miss any slightest detail Mom will get upset. She seems pleased with my observations and I sigh a breath of relief. I greet everyone else, who are already sat outside.

"I didn't think I was late!" I crack a smile that's secretly hiding a panic that maybe I misread the message.

"Not at all, in fact you're ten minutes early!" Mom replies. Phew. These people I swear must do this sort of shit on purpose.

We talk for hours about our lives and everything new that's happened, it really *has* been a while since we've all done this. I tell them about Nicole's travels and Dan getting sacked whilst Jack was defending my honour, I still can't quite believe it! We reminisce a lot about the past too, and growing up. I don't have my pink bear right now to relax me, but I do have Charlie, and he makes the best blanket, he's so soft and warm. Even when talking about uncomfortable things, I still feel content with him around. Maybe I need an emotional support dog. This might sell it to Nicole better. I make another mental note of this; maybe forgetting the pudding one though, if I'm hoping to get my own way.

These people, my people, have helped me out a lot over the years. Saved me from many traumas. I'm forever grateful. And grateful of today too. As I leave, I give everyone a massive hug, I realise this time is precious. This'll be a memory I treasure forever. All of us, all together like this again. Not forgetting the amazing cheesecake, of course – which went down a treat!

***

Once I get home, I realise how quiet it is. I put on the TV as background noise to comfort me. The house is a right mess and I feel so good right now and motivated. So, spring cleaning it is! I've got to make sure it's nice for when Nicole comes home! I pick up a pile of dirty washing and go through the pockets as to not forget anything. I find my letter, folded neatly in a trouser pocket and decide that I'll have another read of it tonight, as Sam suggested, it's got to be worth another try.

Reading it out loud didn't make me feel much different about it, but it definitely got me thinking. I remember what it was like to write music with my friends, spending all our free time jamming and bouncing ideas off each-other. I loved it. I was so inspired back then. I decide to unearth one of our old CD's, which I know is still in a box under my bed. I carefully place it in to my CD player and press play.

As soon as I hear those familiar riffs I realise life wasn't all that bad.

I decide to contact some of my old friends to see if they fancied a catch-up. I figured the loneliness wasn't doing me much good, so I'd better try and get out more, literally. I glance back to the letter and start thinking about 'what if's', which was the problem I had with it before, and decide it's probably a good idea to write a list of the 'what if's' – to get them out of my system.

Chapter Sixteen

Nicole's back! FINALLY. I am SO happy! I gave her the biggest hug when I met her at the airport. I really did make that sign for her too. She laughed and called me a wet wipe. I can't help it if I literally cry at EVERYTHING!

I manage to put on a brave face and carefully avoid any conversation that's going to burst this wonderful bubble of ours. We went out for dinner together at our favourite place, just this small Italian restaurant in the city, to celebrate and talk about her trip. She kept a daily journal, which was a great idea and meant I could read all about her mishaps and funny moments as if I were there too. I really wish I was there with her. I decide to make sure I follow her on the next one if I manage to get my monkey under control. It'll be my new goal.

We spoke about anything and everything else though. It was continuous, as if we'd each saved up every thought and conversation and then released them all over one dinner. She showed me her photos and her favourite monkey family. They were actually very cute, not that I liked to admit out-loud.

***

That evening, Nicole and I meet with Jack and Emili to go bowling. I'm pretty sure none of us are particularly keen on bowling, but Jack was excited for us to get to know Emili better and he always liked the idea of double-dating, so we accepted.

"Ah! Hi Nicole!" Jack jumps up excitedly. "How was your trip?" He bounds over giving her a massive hug. We've barely got through the door, he must been sat literally eagle-eyeing it in anticipation of our arrival.

"Hey Jack, it was INCREDIBLE thank you, I can't wait to tell you all about it!" Nicole bursts. "And this must be Emili?" She gestures to a quite frankly, terrified looking Emili sat looking towards them.

"Ah yes! Nicole, this is my *girlfriend*, Emili!" Jacks emphasis on the word 'girlfriend' makes him sound like a very excited, and very new to dating and relationships in general, teenager. As we walk over to Emili, she stands up and gives a short wave as Nicole goes straight in for a hug. Emili's eyes pop as Nicole presses herself against her and she freezes, stiff.

"Erm, I forgot to mention, Nicole, Emili can be quite anxious meeting new people" Jack starts.

"Yeah, thanks, Jack!" Emili interrupts, almost annoyed, "it's okay." She finishes, addressing Nicole.

"Oh, sorry I had no idea!" Nicole retreats.

"No really, it's okay" Emili repeats, starting to glow red. I know exactly how she feels!

"Anyway" Jack coughs, "and finally" he says, gathering himself, "Emili, this is Nicole, Lou's wife."

"Nice to meet you, I've heard so much about you." She replies dutifully, as if it was rehearsed.

"So, shall we bowl?" Jack suggests, eager to move on. I haven't said a word yet and I feel super awkward. I look over to Emili and smile. She smiles back. I feel like we understand each-other, even without speaking. I wonder how her monkey's behaving right now.

Jack and Nicole haven't stopped talking since we arrived, which is nice, I'm glad my wife and best friend get along so well, they're actually quite similar in a lot of ways. Both so confident and out-going. It's no wonder that Jack ended up with someone more like me, we all balance each-other well.

"So how're things, *really*?" I ask Emili.

"Not too bad thanks, I mean, I worried hellishly about meeting you guys here tonight, if I'm honest. I didn't know if I could do it." She admits.

I look up at her nervous blue eyes, smile and say "me either", and just like that we're laughing.

We continue in lighter conversation and all seems to be going well until...

"She was in a right state to be honest; I've never seen her like it before..."

"JACK!" I interrupt. And realise as I've literally just jumped in and planted myself between them guiltily when really, they could have been talking about ANYTHING; it probably isn't about me at all. But if it is... Ah, I *know* it is. I really should've asked Jack to not mention it beforehand, why didn't I do that, why didn't I THINK?!

"What?" He answers, breaking my unhelpful cycle. I can see everyone's eyes on me, even the people in the next lane. I have no idea who those people are, but feel annoyed at them for being so nosey.

"Erm, yes! Exactly! *'What'*? *What* are you guys, erm, talking about?" I try to act casual, stepping away and slowly sliding myself back on to the bench opposite them, as if they wouldn't notice a thing. Emili looks terrified all over again.

"Just that you were having a bit of a hard time, you know, when Nicole was gone." Jack repeats, sensitively.

Holy fuck, Jack. This cannot be happening. WHY is this happening! Why didn't I just tell Jack to...

"Is it true, Lou?" I see Nicole's eyes become grey with sadness, like that happy bubble has just popped. This is exactly what I *didn't* want to happen. I feel guilty and angry all at once. I don't know how to cope with Nicole's sadness right now, so I address Jack instead, picking up a bowling ball in the process as if nothing's wrong, but my face says everything, my face always gives me away. He looks scared.

"Why are you narking on me, *mate*?" And as the words leave my mouth I passive-aggressively throw the ball down the alley imagining the pins are Jack's head. I hope in doing so that this makes me feel better, using the old 'fake it until you make it' technique, but it doesn't. The anger just carries on building. I can feel my monkey hopping up and down on the spot, like it's sat on a spring, getting gradually higher with every bounce.

"What were you *thinking*? Telling Nicole how shit I've been without her." I begin, starting to shake. My attempt at calming myself down failed. The show must go on, my monkey prepares. "Now she's going to feel like shit for leaving, I don't want her to regret going out and living her dream!" I hear the drums slowly banging, the music's started, my monkey's standing centre-stage waiting, the audience chanting. "She's going to think I can't handle myself whilst she's away! What have you done?" I wail.

Jack looks gobsmacked. Emili is wincing at the whole situation, I'm sure she's hoping for it to end soon. And it will, soon. I can't seem to focus anymore; I've lost all control now. The show has begun. And all I can do is run, run away as fast and as far as I can. I need to escape. I can't breathe.

I leave in a blur and end up sitting on the kerb by my car, sobbing in to my arms, which are crossed over my knees. *All* of my thoughts at this point need challenging, but I haven't got the strength to. All I can do is cry. And wish for this to be over.

"My lovely Louise" I just about hear through all the drumming. I barely twitch. I need her but I don't know how to reach out to her. I feel as if I've left my body altogether, it's possessed by a wild animal (that apparently likes show-business). She sits next to me and puts a hand on my back, gently stroking my nearly soaked-through with sweat, t-shirt. I can still *feel* her.

"I'm here now, why didn't you tell me before?" Nicole helps. I open my mouth but nothing comes out. My shoulders are still shaking as I try to catch my breath through the tears. She hugs me for a few minutes and tries again.

"We don't have to talk about things if you don't want, or are not ready to." She starts. "Shall we get you home?" I nod. I really want to go home.

We get home, she hands me a gin, which completely throws me. Maybe she knows I need it right now. And I tell her everything, including the letter, which I also show her. I sob for about an hour in her arms, until I finally start to feel safe again. My head is throbbing with pain and I think about going to bed. It's a relief that she knows, but the way it all came about was terrible.

There's a solemn knock at the door. It's Jack. It's like he has a sixth sense, like he knows when my gin bottle is open. I'm annoyed at him, but equally impressed. I really don't have the energy left to face him right now, but I know he must be worried. Nicole lets him in, leaves the room and Jack and I begin to talk.

"I was still building up the courage and to talk to her about it all you know..." I begin.

"I know, I know, I wasn't thinking. It wasn't my place to say. But she asked me how you'd *really* been; she must've known something was up with you. And I couldn't *not* tell her. I'm really worried about you, mate." Jack admits.

So she knew all along? Of course she did, just like Jack did. Why do I take these people as fools? I should know better by now. I feel a new twist of guilt and sigh.

"Are things okay between you two?" Jack asks anxiously.

"Of course, yeah, Nicole's been great. I just wish that I'd told her sooner, but it never really seemed the right time. Guess there never really is, is there?" I ask, rhetorically.

"Well, it's good she knows now, and we can all be here for you. What can I do, Lou?" He asks.

"I'm not sure, Jack" I think out-loud. Then an idea hits me. "This might sound a bit weird" I try, "but, will you listen to a letter I wrote to myself?" I finish, close my eyes and wait for him to fall about laughing, but he doesn't.

"Of course", he replies.

Sam was kind of right, reading it out loud to someone, it does hit me differently. Maybe because I'm mildly intoxicated at this point. Maybe not. I decide to go to bed, as all of this just seems surreal now. And with that, I'm out.

Chapter Seventeen

Somehow the air feels different now; people aren't watching their backs in worry of that weasel listening in to their private conversations, twisting what he's heard and then snitching back to the boss. I'm pretty sure she never gave a shit anyway. But I think he amused her nonetheless. So he's gone now and thanks to Jack, Katie's seen the truth. Everyone in the break room is talking about it, and I know this because there's deathly silence when I walk in. Everyone's eyes are on me. I feel like they're waiting for me to perform. My monkey hands me its tambourine out of awkwardness for me. Wow, empathy. It seems to have calmed down a lot since 'that' night. I think I've exhausted it. I've come to realise that, maybe it *isn't* the monkey that causes the chaos in my head; maybe it is just me all along. I decided from that night that I wouldn't give myself such a hard time any more. I don't need it, or deserve it. In a bizarre twist of fate, everyone in the room starts clapping. Did I zone out, perform some sort of ritual for them unknowingly and then zone back in? I start smiling anyway looking around the room, feeling flattered, yet, still unsure why. I even start clapping along with them and take a short, sharp bow, out of courtesy; give the people what they want! They start cheering and I wonder how long this bizarre celebration is going to go on for. All this because I got rid of Dan? But wait, *I* didn't get rid of Dan. That can't be why they're clapping. I'm so confused. I've probably lost it. Yep, that's it, it's done now; I've finally gone cuckoo! Katie walks in and everyone stops, I continue to clap once or twice more in solo, obviously missing the memo, and eventually freeze, with my hands still poised together as I turn to face Katie.

"Can we have a chat?" Katie summons.

Oh shit, yep, this really is it; there will be people with a cuddle jacket waiting for me in her office, waiting to take me away. Sam will be there shaking her head saying how sorry she is that it had to come to this and... No. I'm not doing this anymore, remember? Okay, deep breaths. I walk in, and Katie closes the door behind me, handing me an empty open box in the process. Oh great, I've been sacked, I'm going to be told I need to clear my desk. Damnit. There's silence outside. I can feel everyone waiting in anticipation for my return; I can feel their energy from the lion's den side of the door.

I'm in there a while, so by the time our meeting finished, the break room was nearly empty. I'm in a complete blur though, just concentrating on putting one foot in front of the other. As I continue zombie-footing down towards my office I hear a "well done" and a "yeah, congratulations, Louise!" in the distance. I finally get to the office, sheepishly opening the door and find Jack sat there with a party hat on and single party popper in his hand which he pulls at as I enter. The paper strands fall at my feet and Jack jumps up singing;

"Congratulaaations Assistant Manager!"

I still don't believe it, I'm in complete shock! The clapping kind of makes sense now, but it's crazy that everyone found out before *I* did! Even Jack! The guy even had time to buy a party hat!

"Speech, speech!" I hear Jack request. After a few moments, I feel like I'm finally present in the room and start to smile. My cheeks are warming and I feel a surge of excitement building up inside me, I feel like I could actually burst!

"What a dream come true, I never thought this could happen to me, I'm so happy I could cry! I'd like to thank my Mom, my Dad..!" I joke. We both fall about laughing. This is all *totally* insane.

I realise I'm still holding on to the box Katie gave me, even though I told her I wouldn't be needing it, I'd rather stay with Jack than have my own, lonely bit of space. She was understanding of this, thankfully.

"What's the box for, are you leaving me?" His voice shakes.

"I'm not going *anywhere*." I declare, throwing the box towards the waste bin heroically and missing terribly.

So not only am I now 'Assistant Manager' with more holiday entitlement and better pay, but I also have my own budget to 'play' with, which I can use to bring my idea to life! I wonder when this information will sink in, and as I do, I think about what I'm going to wear tonight, as obviously, this causes for celebration! I must text *the girls* right away! I instantly pick up my phone and compose a message for our group chat, aptly named 'the girls', and invite them all out for a boozy night. I already can't wait to see them; my four *other* best friends. 'My people.'

Chapter Eighteen

"Okay, I've got it now, so this one?" I ask, holding up a sparkly grey dress up against me. "Or this one?" I suggest, holding up a similar-styled sequin skirt and plain cream top in the other hand. Nicole's shaking her head which is now sagged and balancing in her palm.

"You've been through your *whole* wardrobe now Lou, please make a decision." She sighs looking at the room, covered in my clothing. She's lost all interest now and I don't blame her. I have been doing this a while. But I'm so happy and tonight is so important to me, I don't often celebrate, because I don't often do anything worth celebrating. This is a big deal to me! I decide to go with the dress; it looks more 'party' than the other finalist.

I throw it on, along with some subtle eye-liner and lipstick and skip towards the door, Nicole in close pursuit, I guess in case I change my mind. I bet she never thought we'd actually leave!

***

"Hey guys!" I squeal. "It's been so long, how is everyone?" I look around and see a bunch of familiar faces, there's Kloe, not my longest, but certainly my best female friend. We met in high-school, and spent every possible moment together. She's the most non-judgmental person I have ever met, the sort of person that you can one-hundred-percent just be yourself around. She's stuck with me through some pretty shitty times. I trust her with my life. I should definitely make more of an effort to see her.

Then there's Kat, the crazy one. Everyone has a 'crazy one', right? Well, Kat is mine. She's absolutely nuts. We have such a laugh together; we bonded over photography and old barrel cider at a college exhibition. Obviously the cider wasn't provided, but the college foolishly set it up in an old brewery, to be all 'edgy' and stuff. But really it was a great excuse to get drunk and meet new, like-minded people.

Next is Lucie, who is my oldest friend, I've known her for god knows how long, since the beginning of time, I think. Lucie was always really quiet in school and I think I was the only person that used to try and talk to her. In all honesty, she was my first crush, even though I didn't realise it at the time. She was super interesting and kind of mysterious. Lucie has an amazing amount of patience and she's really supportive, I'm lucky to have her as a friend still after all these years.

And lastly, there's Maddie; who I've known the least amount of time, but when we met we connected right away. I met Maddie through work, not at the factory, but at my previous job, when I was a waitress. She helped me out big time when I dropped (and smashed) a whole crate of milk bottles. She also stopped me from bitching about the manager when he was walking up right behind me and oh, I can't forget the time I nearly spilt hot gravy all down some poor man's crotch and she swooped in to save me just in time. I used to be pretty clumsy. Luckily, he didn't really notice. She's a hero. Everyone needs a Maddie in their life.

"I've missed you all so much!" I can't help but let out.

"We've missed you too, Lou!" Lucie smiles.

"Yeah for sure, been way too long mate," chimes in Kat.

"Anyway, ladies, let's not forget to make a toast" Kloe leads. "To Louise and her promotion!" She lifts a glass and everyone else, including myself, also raise our champagne glasses to the air, making sure to all tap each other's in unison and hearing various beautiful chiming tones as we do. This is so fancy, I hardly ever have champagne. I take a sip and savour the moment.

"Thanks, everyone, it really means a lot." I sob. I catch Nicole looking at me, smiling with pride. I feel so happy right now.

We talk in to the long hours about all the times we had together through school, sixth form and becoming young adults. We all had our challenges, but we had each other too, which definitely helped. Each of the girls start to leave, I say goodbye to Kat, Lucie and then Kloe. And I'm left now with Maddie and Nicole. Maddie's barely said a word all night, which is unlike her, but there wasn't an awful lot of opportunity to get a word in, there rarely is when we all get together!

"How're you doing anyways, Mads, you seemed quiet tonight?" I hiccup. Definitely an alccup at this point though, as Jack would say! Jack is a huge fan of putting words together, he especially loves 'hangry', a mix of hungry and angry, and 'bromance', a splice of brother and romance. 'Alccup' is his very own creation and a merge of alcohol and hiccups. I quietly chuckle to myself. He's a funny guy.

"I'm actually doing really well, thanks Lou. I mean, there *was* something I wanted to talk about tonight, but I guess I was too afraid to when it actually came to it. Maybe that's why?" She admits.

"Oh no, Maddie! I'm sorry; we never really gave you a chance to, with our constant nattering! Did you want to talk about it now?" I encourage.

"I guess it's easier to now, with just you guys, as I know *you'll* both understand, anyway." She starts.

My mind is spinning with curiosity and I can see Nicole's is doing the same. "It's just that, I've realised this thing and I've been thinking about it for some time now and I just need to get it out." She continues, making hand gestures that indicate pulling something literally off her chest. Nicole and I look at each other; I think we've worked it out. I grab Maddie's hand and smile.

"It's okay, Mads" I manage.

"Yeah, we totally get it." Nicole adds.

"You want to go back to school and re-do your A-Levels because your results were a bit shit and you want to get a better job than the one you have now as a cold caller!" I finish.

"NO!" Maddie nearly shouts, pulling her hand away, "you couldn't be *more* wrong!" Maddie looks hurt.

"Yeah, Lou, *so* wrong!" Nicole concurs, although looking as bloody confused as I am - she's none the wiser! 'Whose side are you on' I try to transmit to her in hope she can suddenly start to mind-read.

"My job *is* shit..." Maddie finally agrees, "But it's not that at all. And by the way, I'm *not* a cold caller. I'm a debt collector."

"Of course, yeah, sorry, so what is it then?" I push, in hope that she still wants to confide in me.

"Well, I... I'm bisexual." She confesses. "I like men, and women."

"Ah, bloody greedy then?" I snort. I make jokes when I don't know how to respond appropriately. But this one doesn't go down too well.

"No, Louise, just because like both genders doesn't mean that I'm a slut." She spits. "I thought you of all people would understand how difficult it is to come out. Why are you making a joke out of it?"

"I'm sorry, Maddie." I see the error in my response and dwell quietly for a moment. "I guess it's because, well, yeah, I *do* know how difficult it is to come out. It was hard for me, and I guess that's why I joke about it now, to lighten it up. It was the most daunting thing I ever had to do. It's a shame in this day and age that we even have to 'come out' any more. I mean, people shouldn't assume you're straight!" I save.

"So true", Nicole agrees. "My parents didn't get it straight away; I think they thought it was some sort of 'phase' that I'd out-grow. My friends were great though, they were pretty cool about the whole thing. I was lucky."

I notice Maddie's face, filled with relief, searching our faces for support. "I love you mate, I'm glad you told us." I reward, proudly.

**

What a night. I really am so proud of Maddie. It was kind of inspiring! She was braver than I was. I remember when I came out, I'd gotten myself in to a depression from denial and I withdrew from everyone. I was afraid of rejection and pain, so I thought hiding it would be the safest thing to do. In the end though, I was forced to come out, as some kids heard about it in school and I didn't want it to get back to my parents that way. So I wrote it all in a letter to my Mom. I sat next to her whilst she read it, but I couldn't bear to look her in the eye. I felt embarrassed and ashamed. She wrote me a letter back, expressing how relieved she was; as she knew I was hiding something, but didn't know what. She said that she assumed I was on drugs, which is why she was so relieved to find out it wasn't. Despite being a bit annoyed she'd think so poorly of me, I was also relieved that it was all out in the open. My long over-due secret was finally revealed and my family were all fine with it. The kids at school on the other hand, weren't quite as accepting. School really was hard for me. The boys thought it was hilarious, like I was a walking, talking joke who made them all laugh out loud just at the very sight of me, and the girls believed I was some sort of a sexual predator out to get them. I had to tell them numerous times that just because I liked girls didn't mean that I fancied *all* of them. And as if I'd fancy any of *them*, they were horrible people! I remember always purposely trying to be late for P.E. so that I could avoid getting changed next to them. I made that mistake once - never again. They'd say things like 'ergh the lesbian's looking at me, ergh she fancies me.' 'Don't flatter yourselves' I'd reply, but standing up for myself always seemed to make the bullying worse.

I guess because my self-esteem was so low after this experience – what with all the name calling, the laughing... Being treated as someone that was below everyone else, like I didn't matter; like it didn't matter if I existed (it really was a dark time). It's no wonder that I ended up in unhealthy relationships for a short while after. That became my 'norm', and it took a long time to forgive myself and move on. After all, I did nothing wrong. I had to stop punishing myself for simply being me. Enough is enough. I'm proud of myself for coming out the other end. Good job I had a lot of good people around me too, to show me the way back.

As I mull over my difficult past, I find my old pink bear out from under the blankets of my bed and give him a squeeze, my head resting on his, and I sigh heavily with relief and gratitude that I'm here now, living a much healthier and happier life.

Chapter Nineteen

I'm sat, at my old familiar desk (thank god I didn't have to move), with a blank pad of paper hungrily facing me, waiting for me to satisfy it with ideas. Time to get started. I take a deep breath in and become mindful of this moment. This is the moment I'd been waiting for. To be heard, to be appreciated.

"Well, come on then!" I jump at the voice suddenly in my ear. I can feel Jacks breath on me.

"Jack, get away, what are you doing?" I demand.

"I'm so excited for you to get started, what will you do first? What's your vision? Where's it going?" He responds, excitedly.

"You're as bad as I am!" I chuckle. "To be honest, I have absolutely no idea!" I realise as I say it out loud.

But eventually, I re-find my inspiration and get to work. I fill most of the pad in one morning, Jack watching on in awe, handing me the occasional brew as payment for allowing him to watch the show. Not that I'm particularly 'allowing' him, I don't really have a choice in the matter.

"This is looking so good, Lou!" He can't help but butt in with glee.

The office phone starts ringing. Normally I dread it - even worse if I let it ring out. I'm waiting for that horrible feeling to pang me, but it doesn't. I then realise that I haven't seen or heard anything of my monkey for a little while. It's strange, but I've kind of missed it, like it was a fairy godmother or something, but it really wasn't. Maybe this is me getting better.

"Are you going to answer that?" Jack chirps.

"Oh yeah, yeah, of course." I reply, snapping out of my day-dream.

"Hello, Louise Grainger" I answer.

"Hi Louise, it's Katie. Just checking-in, how's your first day going? Do you need anything from me?"

Do I need anything from *her*? Shouldn't it be; what does she need from *me*?!

"Oh, hi Katie!" I turn around, mouthing *'oh my god'* to Jack, who's now running on the spot and clapping his hands together very fast, but very quietly. "I don't think so, I seem to be getting on okay at the moment, but thank you, I appreciate that!"

"No problem, well if you do, you know where I am" she reassures me, and swiftly hangs up.

Jesus, Katie just rang our office! She *never* calls us; she normally gets a minion to do it. That was surreal!

"You're important now, remember Lou! She must really respect you, you've got this." Jack says, responding to my facial expression.

I look down at my pad and read the words;

'Bespoke beauty. It's in your hands, for your hands.'

I have *so* got this.

Chapter Twenty

On reflection, I've come to realise that I haven't had much closure from all the events in my life I want to forget. I guess that's exactly why it *is* so hard to forget; these events have changed me as a person. But in the end, I'm glad that they did. Everything worked out as it should've, as fate intended. I feel more like 'me' than I ever have before. So with that, I don't want to forget where I've come from, and all the challenges I've had to face. It's made me who I am today.

The letter I was advised to write worked out really well too. I realised in writing it, that I'd created a map and all I had to do was work out how to (literally!) read it for it all to make sense. By reading it again, out loud, and to someone else, it forced me to face all the events that I found difficult to process at the time. I'm still not 'cured', but I'm definitely on the right track now, heading in the right direction. I'm so grateful to Nicole and all of my family and friends, but most of all to Jack.

My plans back at the factory went down REALLY well and two years on, I've finally managed to set up my own business! I'm now doing my dream job

— designing! I even hired Maddie as my PA. She much prefers it to debt collecting. Jack and Nicole are also working for me, as Sales Reps, putting their confidence to good use!

Jack and Emili are doing really well and are planning on getting married next year — He's just asked me to be his best wo-man! Which of course I accepted! He is going to have *the* craziest stag do.

Nicole and I are also planning our next adventure — this time we're going to India! I'm so excited about it; I can't wait to experience it all with her. I'm not leaving myself behind this time! And maybe I can wait just a *few* more years for a canine companion!

And I see much less of my monkey now, it's doing what it should be doing and only really surfaces when I need it to, and it seems to be okay with that too, we're at peace now. The very thought of that makes me smile contently to myself and can almost *feel* it patting my back like it's agreeing with what a good job I've done. I imagine it's probably planted a 'kick me' sign on it though, and this makes me laugh. Well, I guess, they are, after all, just monkey tricks!